HOLY CROSS

and

D0096203

CHRISTIAN EDUCATION

James B. King, C.S.C.

AVE MARIA PRESS AVE Notre Dame, Indiana

Founded in 1865, Ave Maria Press is a ministry of the United States Province of Holy Cross.

www.avemariapress.com

Paperback: ISBN-13 978-1-59471-663-8

E-book: ISBN-13 978-1-59471-664-5

Cover image © Thinkstock.

Cover design by Kristen Hornyak Bonelli.

Text design by David Scholtes.

Printed and bound in the United States of America.

CONTENTS

∽

FOREWORD

∽

Dear Friends,

This booklet is an attempt to distill the essential elements that typically characterize Holy Cross's educational ministries across the globe, including at the University of Notre Dame, the University of Portland, Stonehill College, King's College, St. Edward's University, Holy Cross College, and the many Holy Cross secondary schools around the world. As noted in the text, the bonds that students, faculty, staff, and alumni experience at these schools are ultimately the product of Blessed Basil Moreau's original vision for Holy Cross education. That familial atmosphere first manifested itself at Notre Dame de Sainte-Croix, the first school Moreau founded in 1836 in Le Mans, France, and though sometimes difficult to define, it is easily perceived wherever one encounters the community in the world today.

Virtually all religious orders have at some point needed to "rediscover" their founders, and in the last several decades, the legacy and writings of Fr. Moreau have been mined ever more effectively to reveal his practical pastoral genius and farsighted educational philosophy. To some extent, Moreau's influence has not been sufficiently appreciated because he left behind no lengthy, systematic treatment of his thoughts on Catholic education. Nevertheless, the charism he entrusted to the Congregation continues to strongly influence its own members and make the educational ministries where it serves distinctive.

As proud as we are of Holy Cross sisters, brothers, and priests who have devoted their lives to the educational ministry, we are also indebted to so many of our lay collaborators who carry on the spirit of Fr. Moreau in Holy Cross schools throughout the world. Together, as his sons and daughters, we continue the tradition of "educating the mind while cultivating the heart," the true holistic model of a Holy Cross education.

Yours in Holy Cross,
Rev. Thomas J. O'Hara, C.S.C.
Provincial Superior
Congregation of Holy Cross,
United States Province of Priests and Brothers

INTRODUCTION

❧

Blessed Basil Anthony Moreau, the founder of the Congregation of Holy Cross, was born in Laigné-en-Belin, a small village about nine miles south of Le Mans, France, on February 11, 1799. He was the ninth of fourteen children born to Louise and Louis Moreau, owners of a small wine shop. They were simple folk, most likely illiterate, and pious Catholics. Though their children had to work from a young age in the shop and in fields the family tended, the Moreaus, uncharacteristically for the times, forswore corporal punishment; exclusion from family prayer was the ultimate punishment in their household. Moreau's parents were the most formative influence upon his faith and character, and he remained extraordinarily devoted to them and to his siblings throughout his life.

Nine months after Moreau's birth, Napoleon Bonaparte took power and put an end to the French Revolution, which had begun in 1789 when King Louis XVI was forced to abdicate amid popular discontent with his bloated regime. Nobles gorged themselves at the public trough, oblivious to the growing wealth gap between rich and poor. Commoners grew increasingly restless as their taxes were raised to support a series of costly wars and to maintain the inefficient state bureaucracy. At the same time, historical notions that kings' authority came from God and their personages were inherently divine in nature had been undermined by Enlightenment ideas that promoted individual rights, self-government, and skepticism about religion.

While many priests were themselves impoverished, the Catholic Church collectively owned about one-tenth of France's land and enjoyed a host of legal and financial privileges accumulated over centuries, including freedom from taxation. Some clergy, especially among the lower ranks, initially supported the Revolution, hoping it would redress legitimate grievances, but anticlerical extremists soon gained control. Within a decade most of the Church's property was confiscated, monasteries and convents were closed, religious orders were outlawed, and all clergy were required to take an oath of allegiance to the state. After assuming power at the end of the century, Napoleon permitted the Church to be reconstituted, though under more restrictive norms than had existed previously.

Many Catholics during the 1790s, particularly in rural areas, remained loyal to underground clergy who refused to take the oath. Small networks of peasants risked their own lives to shield and hide priests on farms and in forests where they lived under threat of arrest, deportation, beatings, and even the guillotine. They would gather together, sometimes in barns or cellars with friends standing watch, to celebrate the Eucharist and other sacraments secretly with clergy who surfaced at irregular intervals. With France's government wracked by chronic instability and its people's loyalties divided, the degree of religious persecution varied over time and region depending upon the sympathies of local authorities and the whims of their superiors in Paris.

Nevertheless, Moreau's parents ensured that their son was baptized by a priest who had refused to take the oath. After Napoleon assumed power, the new pastor of the parish adjoining the Moreau home was also one of those who had exercised his ministry clandestinely for years. By that time the French educational system, which had been administered almost wholly by the Church, including 321 schools in the Diocese of Le Mans alone, was virtually destroyed. While persecution against the Church generally abated as Moreau was growing up, resentments still simmered below the surface and occasionally spiked.

When he was ordained a priest a full generation later in 1821, his homeland and the Church were slowly recovering. Religious schools began to open again, along with new secular ones, but his was virtually a lost generation. Young people of his age in many parts of France were left mostly uneducated and largely uncatechized as literacy rates plunged. Civil servants well into the nineteenth century tended to be anticlerical and used a variety of quasi-legal and bureaucratic means to impede the Church's educational ministry during the recovery. Instead of permanently settling the relationship between Church and state, the Napoleonic reforms continued to provoke difficulties for decades afterward, especially for Catholic religious orders still prohibited from directly owning land or property.

Moreau spent his childhood years watching the Church struggle to regain its footing and sustain itself against lingering discrimination that ranged from selective and subtle to nakedly overt. Those childhood memories left an indelible imprint upon him. He later came to see that his major purposes as a priest and educator were to evangelize adult Catholics so they understood the basic principles of their faith and to provide the young with a first-rate liberal arts education that would enable them to surmount antireligious prejudice and so gain the capacity to transform civil society in the decades ahead.

As Moreau grew into his teens both very bright and exceedingly pious, his pastor keenly perceived within him a potential vocation to the priesthood. Whatever may have been lacking in his own early education, he quickly grasped complex subjects, eventually becoming an excellent student in philosophy and theology. Yet as Moreau navigated his way through seminary studies, he increasingly saw possibilities beyond the needs and circumstances of his native region and petitioned his bishop to send him to a seminary for foreign missionaries. At this early age, he wanted to be sent, like the first apostles, to spread faith in Jesus Christ and his Good News where he was most needed.

However, his superiors had already slated him for advanced studies and training as a seminary professor. Moreau dedicated himself to serving obediently in this role and became a popular instructor, respected not only for the clarity of his lectures but also for his personal piety and pastoral energy. He quickly developed a reputation throughout the diocese of Le Mans as an excellent preacher and was frequently called upon to assist at parishes and give retreats.

Moreau might have become a prominent theologian had he focused upon developing his scholarship. Instead, he spent many years as a student and professor formulating a rich spirituality based predominantly upon imitating the person of Jesus that he ended up applying practically in the communities and ministries he established.

Sixteen years after he was ordained a priest, Moreau became the founder of the Congregation of Holy Cross, whose members he sent out across France and as missionaries around the world. The Congregation was provisionally formed through the "Fundamental Act of Union" signed on March 1, 1837. Through this pact, Moreau succeeded in combining into a single association two groups of religious: a small number of auxiliary priests he had gathered two years earlier from among the diocesan ranks to preach parish missions and instruct youth; and the Brothers of St. Joseph, a loose confederation of teaching brothers founded by Rev. Jacques Dujarié in 1820.

Dujarié had nearly become a martyr during the height of the Revolution's terror. He traveled in disguise to be ordained secretly in Paris and, like Moreau's childhood pastor, was protected by an underground network of loyal Catholics when a warrant was issued for his arrest. He spent his first years as a priest moving stealthily from one rural hiding spot to another. In the early 1800s he became a pastor and founded the Sisters of Providence in the western region of Ruillé-sur-Loir; more than a decade later, he founded the Brothers of St. Joseph, but by the early 1830s his health was failing and the number of brothers had declined by almost half. He turned to Moreau for guidance and after several years demonstrated his trust in the younger man by relinquishing authority over the Brothers to him. Dujarié gave his blessing to Moreau's proposal to merge the two associations into one and died a year later in 1838.

One biographer states that as Moreau matured, "there burned within him an ardor which was ceaselessly aflame along with a compelling necessity to undertake and to resurrect projects lying on the verge of ruin and to bring into existence others which were destined to live."[1] The Association of Holy Cross, as Moreau's new organization was originally named, was the ultimate manifestation of both tendencies. Under Dujarié only a few brothers had taken religious vows and then only for a year at a time. Many brothers and priests were initially skeptical of joining together into a common association and some of the brothers left after Moreau undertook his reforms. It took another decade for all of the members to commit themselves to lifelong poverty, chastity, and obedience.

In 1836, Moreau purchased land from a friend and moved his enterprise to an area known as Sainte-Croix (Holy Cross), which then lay on the outskirts of Le Mans. The community is, in fact, named after this neighborhood, though many people understandably though incorrectly add an article and refer to the Congregation of *the* Holy Cross. Moreau certainly did not object that his association was inevitably identified closely with the Cross of Jesus. Notre Dame de Sainte-Croix, the Congregation's first primary school, was established there, and a secondary school or "college" added in 1838. Moreau also founded a community of religious women at Sainte-Croix, the Marianites, one of three sisters' congregations that would eventually bear the name of Holy Cross.

As his vision of religious life evolved, it is no surprise that he dedicated each branch of his community to a particular person in the Holy Family whose virtues were to be imitated: the brothers to St. Joseph, the priests to Christ, and the sisters to the Blessed Virgin Mary. Moreau wrote a good deal about the importance for all religious of imitating the example of Jesus, and he constantly exhorted them to remain united with one another like the original disciples as reported in the Acts of the Apostles. Nevertheless, the ultimate purpose of his religious family was rooted in a commitment to evangelization and education, whether that meant leading former parishioners back to the Church in France or bringing people to the faith for the first time in foreign lands.

In 1856, Moreau published a short work titled *Christian Education* that addresses the purposes of Catholic schools, discusses the essential qualities needed by teachers, and provides practical advice about how teachers should manage their classes and relationships with students. Although it lay virtually neglected even within the Congregation for a century after Moreau's death, over the last several decades it has increasingly become a seminal source for understanding the distinctive educational charism that he bequeathed to Holy Cross. The first sentence of Moreau's small booklet states, "[Education] is the art of forming youth—that is to say, for a Christian, to make of youth people who are con-formed to Jesus Christ, their model."[2] Moreau believed that life was essentially a personal, daily struggle for union with God in which the Christian modeled himself after the Son's example of fidelity. While none of us can be quite so perfect, the aim for the Christian was twofold: to reach one's fullest potential in this world while remaining focused upon the ultimate goal of fullness in the life to come.

Moreau wanted Sainte-Croix to be an institution that excelled academically but was also spiritually formative in the Catholic faith, one where students consciously strove, much like members of his religious community, to imitate the ideal of the Holy Family and be a sign of the true com-munion possible with God. As the years have unfolded and Holy Cross has delved deeper into *Christian Education* and other writings of its founder, a form of pedagogy emerges that accurately reflects the process by which a child grad-ually evolves into an adult. It is a vision that takes young people from their earliest days of grappling with ideas and making sense of the world around them to preparing them through formation in faith and values for lifelong disciple-ship in a supportive environment that nourishes their gifts and fuels their desire for God. The five principles described here capture the recurring themes in Moreau's writings that continue to shape the lives of students in Holy Cross educational institutions today, wherever they are located throughout the world:

Mind
seeking understanding
through the integration of
faith and reason

Heart
discerning one's personal
vocation in service to the
Church and world

Zeal
enkindling the desire to
use one's gifts to boldly
proclaim God's Word

Family
embracing Christian
community as the context
for lifelong formation

Hope
trusting in the Cross and
God's promise of the
kingdom

MIND

❧

Even though we base our philosophy
course on the data of faith, no one
need fear that we shall confine our
teaching within narrow and unscientific boundaries. No, we wish to
accept science without prejudice and
in a manner adapted to the needs of
our times. We do not want our students to be ignorant of anything they
should know. To this end, we shall
shrink from no sacrifice.

—*Basil Moreau: Essential Writings*, 417

A Holy Cross education begins with a rigorous and full
development of the mind. Moreau himself was a committed student who took his studies seriously and engaged
energetically in intellectual controversies and debates. While
a student and young priest, he was disciplined in his studies
and motivated to do extra reading and linguistic studies
in addition to assigned course work. After his ordination,
he went on for postgraduate studies in Paris and a decade
later paid for several other priests to do the same at his own
expense. He took the initiative to correspond with leading
intellectuals, seeking both insights and opportunities for
dialogue with them. Moreau was known for quoting Bacon

and Cicero alongside Aquinas and other theologians, and he added the first science course, a class in physics, to the seminary curriculum in Le Mans in 1835.

Moreau perceived early on that it was detrimental to both the Church and society for Catholics to disengage from the scholarly questions and controversies of the age. He was a contemporary of Cardinal John Henry Newman and may have been familiar with his writings. Moreau would certainly have appreciated the cardinal's observation that "nature pursues its course, now coincident with that of grace, now parallel to it, now across, now divergent, now counter, in proportion to its own imperfection and to the attraction and influence which grace exerts over it."[3] Both Moreau and Newman fully believed that grace and nature are complementary sources of God's revelation and integral to human understanding. However, as the Industrial and Scientific Revolutions advanced, both men recognized that the tension between the dogmas and interests of the Church and those of society was increasingly straining the traditional historical understanding in Christian Europe that ultimate truth emanates from the Creator.

While neither man's beliefs were shaken by new discoveries like the scientific theory of natural selection that caused others to doubt the very existence of God, they each recognized the danger of the trend since the onset of Enlightenment to compartmentalize theology and rely solely upon human knowledge. Consequently, Moreau, like Newman, intensified his efforts to promote the kind of Christian education that would more authentically assert the Church's conviction that true knowledge and understanding inevitably rest upon the integration of reason and faith.

More than a decade before Charles Darwin published *On the Origin of Species*, Moreau welcomed the positive contributions of scientific learning to an extent that would still be provoking controversy within some quarters of the Church decades later. Nearly seventy years before the outbreak of World War I, Moreau forecast that the tumults periodically rocking post-Revolutionary France were but a prelude of worse things to come: "It is not hard to foresee an imminent and radical change in the destinies of all Europe, and even of the entire human race."[4] The need to instill in young people the capacity to understand and deal with the societal conflicts that simmered below the surface of post-Enlightenment European culture and would eventually lead to World War I was integral to Moreau's vision.

As he fought for Holy Cross schools to gain acceptance and credibility, Moreau realized that the students who graduated from them would need to be theologically articulate, intellectually proficient, highly skilled scholars and debaters who could hold their ground on others' turf. It was simply essential for the next generation of Christians, including teachers, priests, and religious, to be conversant with modern theories and philosophies, even those they opposed. In fact, Sainte-Croix quickly evolved into a premier school for both primary and high school-aged pupils. Less than a decade after its founding, independent state inspectors, who were frequently biased against Catholic institutions, ranked it ahead of its primary secular competitor, the Royal

College of Le Mans. This was despite local authorities' persistent attempts to deny Moreau permission to teach subjects that would permit the school to be accredited on an equal footing. He had witnessed the same battle throughout his childhood—a struggle which continues to this day in the Church's attempts to refute a variety of ideologies fueled by secularism.

In striving for academic excellence, a Holy Cross education seeks to develop students' intellectual capacities within the context of a broad curriculum. Today, when the prevailing trend in higher education is toward reducing core requirements, the Congregation's colleges and universities remain committed to providing a strong liberal arts foundation, with philosophy and theology courses required for all students in order to equip them for wide, generous engagement with society and culture. That kind of intellectual formation also creates possibilities for more interdisciplinary study and integrative research, in contrast to a movement within many academic disciplines toward increasing specialization and fragmentation of knowledge.

From Moreau's first victory at Sainte-Croix to the present day, the Congregation's schools have been renowned for forming students academically according to the convictions he espoused. The University of Notre Dame is the premier Catholic research institution in the world. The University of Portland is one of the leading regional universities in the western United States. Notre Dame College in Dhaka, Bangladesh, a country that is only 0.3 percent Christian, is widely accepted to be the country's best college, a place where Muslim government ministers readily send their children. Even though Holy Cross College in Agartala, India, was only founded in 2009, it has already earned a reputation for academic excellence, with its underprivileged students achieving success rates on a par with peer institutions. St. George's College (a K–12 school) in Santiago, Chile, has for decades ranked among the nation's elite, and Lakeview Secondary School in Jinja, Uganda, achieved a similar ranking, like Sainte-Croix, within several years of its founding in 1993.

Any fears Moreau had about science trumping religion in the post-Enlightenment era may seem primitive today, as branches of knowledge and technological progress have mushroomed. He would naturally be surprised and shocked by the atomic bomb, moon landing, and cloning. He would probably be delighted with email and iPhones since so many of his problems with distant missions resulted from long lag times between the arrival of handwritten letters carried by clipper ships to France and America. But the speed and complexity of twenty-first-century life would undoubtedly have given him an even greater appreciation for the need to educate and prepare Christians to resist the temptation to put ultimate faith in the promises of science. He would be just as insistent that Christians place themselves in the midst of the debate about how to use the things we produce not only for material or personal gain but ethically and spiritually, for the advancement of all people.

HEART

∽

We shall never forget that virtue, as
Bacon puts it, is the spice which preserves science. We shall always place
education side by side with instruction; the mind will not be cultivated
at the expense of the heart. While we
prepare useful citizens for society, we
shall likewise do our utmost to prepare citizens for heaven.

—*Basil Moreau: Essential Writings*, 417

Human beings can absorb a boundless amount of
knowledge and information, but if Christians fail to
see themselves first as people with a vocation to open their
hearts to Christ, then they cannot expect to change society.
As the current *Constitutions of the Congregation of Holy Cross*
state, "For the kingdom to come in this world, disciples must
have the competence to see and the courage to act."[5] Competence can be acquired externally in many different ways,
but courage is instilled over time by cultivating one's heart
and constantly directing its purposes beyond one's self. It
is a process that requires spiritual and vocational formation
from devoted teachers and other role models. In discovering the truth of who we are as human creatures with social
obligations, born with an innate desire to love and be loved,

we are freed and empowered to become something better, more like the person of Jesus. By cultivating the heart, we develop in virtue and acquire the steadfastness to stand in the face of opposition and derision for the sake of our most deeply held beliefs and hew to a higher standard of justice.

Holy Cross's founder purposefully dedicated a year of his life shortly after ordination to work on cultivating virtue within himself at a nearby monastery. He undoubtedly felt the influence of a wise spiritual advisor who counseled him, "Our first rule must be to disregard what only tickles the ears; it is hearts that we must win."[6] As he progressed from professor and administrator to founder of a religious community, Moreau became convinced that a Holy Cross education should enlighten the heart as well as the mind.

The unfolding of a Christian's baptismal identity over time depends upon discovering the deepest stirrings of one's heart. Moreau preached a sermon in 1833 in which he said, "What must we do to become perfect? Follow Jesus Christ, that is to say, imitate him; that is the commitment we made in baptism. . . . Following Jesus is the consequence of this sacrament of faith; it is the holy and irrevocable law of our vocation to Christianity, and we renew it by our religious promises."[7] It is possible to intellectually grasp and appreciate Jesus' teachings, but they will never become the basis for our actions unless we are compelled by a desire to live and teach from the heart.

Holy Cross colleges and universities today continue to place a particular emphasis on the cultivation of students' hearts through spiritual and vocational formation that builds on the grace of our initiation into the Church. This formation certainly centers upon the celebration of the sacraments—especially the Eucharist, which was Moreau's lifeblood—but it is not confined to chapels and campus ministries. It also takes place in service learning centers, classrooms, and residence halls. Fr. James Connerton, C.S.C., the founding president of King's College in Wilkes-Barre, Pennsylvania, put it quite succinctly when he said that the school's goal was to teach its students "not only how to make a living, but how to live."[8]

Moreau perceived the essential challenge that lay ahead for the Church as the sciences became divorced from their roots in theology, and he sought to shape students in the conviction that their thirst for eternal life must guide their learning and behavior in this life. He had benefited personally from educational opportunities that eluded all but a few among his peers. He had developed his intellect into a powerful means for communicating the Gospel to disparate audiences from seminarians to poor country folk who could not sign their names, and he believed it was his mission to do the same for all, according to each person's abilities. He was convinced that Holy Cross schools should produce graduates who would be more than mere participants—they would be Christian leaders and citizens wherever they found themselves later on.

More than a century after Moreau's death, Pope John Paul II wrote that a Catholic university "enables [students] to acquire, or if they have already done so, to deepen a Christian way of life that is authentic. They should realize the responsibility of their professional life, the enthusiasm of being the trained 'leaders' of tomorrow, of being witnesses to Christ in whatever place they may exercise their profession."[9] A truly Catholic education today, as in Moreau's time, encourages students and faculty to see knowledge and truth as constituting a united and organic whole that is not merely an end in itself.

Moreau never turned on a computer or rode in an automobile, nor did he found a modern college or university. He would not live to see how his educational philosophy would need to be developed further for a much more complex world, and he did not attempt a more complete exposition about the essential harmony between faith and reason as did Cardinal Newman and later Pope John Paul II. However, he intuitively grasped that the empirical and theoretical knowledge acquired by brilliant minds could best be applied for the benefit of the world by citizens whose hearts incline toward God.

ZEAL

∼9

The spirit of faith inspires and animates zeal, that is to say, the sacred fire which the Divine Master came to bring on earth.

—1858 *Rules of the Congregation*

In *Christian Education*, Moreau wrote, "If at times you show preference to any young person, it should be the poor, those who have no one else to show them preference, those who have the least knowledge, those who lack skills and talent, and those who are not Catholic or Christian. If you show them greater care and concern, it must be because their needs are greater and it is only just to give more to those who have received less."[10] In 1844, six years after Sainte-Croix opened its doors and barely a decade after Frédéric Ozanam had founded the Society of Saint Vincent DePaul, Moreau encouraged his students to found one of the society's first school chapters. A couple of years later when sections of Le Mans were inundated by floods, he organized a relief drive and delivered supplies personally by rowboat. Moreau frequently found jobs for the unemployed and took in many of the poor children of the city at the request of city officials.

Consequently, it is not surprising that Holy Cross institutions have been known for instilling a commitment to service in their students and have been innovators in the creation of programs that provide them with multiple opportunities to engage in life-changing domestic and international programs. These continue to grow. Some recent examples include an eleven-month extension program started in 2009 by Stonehill College for postgraduate students that quickly expanded to India, the Dominican Republic, and Honduras; as well as immersion experiences sponsored by Holy Cross College (in Ghana) and St. Edward's University (in Peru, Uganda, and India). These initiatives are characteristic of the spirit that Moreau inculcated in his Sainte-Croix charges, confident that a society increasingly dubious about the dogmatic truths of the Church could be persuaded by the Christian example of those trained to defend its teachings and to fashion their hearts after the person of Christ, our first and greatest teacher.

He also noted in *Christian Education*, "Zeal is the great desire to make God known, loved, and served, and thus to bring knowledge of salvation to others. Activity flows from this virtue."[11] Zeal is what drives and motivates Christians, beginning with their Baptism, to use their gifts and talents for the betterment of others. Zeal fuels us to overcome fear and sacrifice our preferences for the needs of our brothers and sisters when mere human logic fails and we find ourselves compelled to follow the truer impulses of our hearts. As Moreau said succinctly in the mid-1850s, "We are committed by our vocation to extend the reign of Jesus Christ in the hearts of all people."[12]

For Moreau, zeal expresses the virtue that actualizes the development of our minds and the cultivation of our hearts for the good of others. It is the passion to act upon what we have witnessed and learned in classrooms and in our experiences outside of them. An education of mind and heart means to enkindle within students a burning desire to act boldly, like the original disciples, afire with the Holy Spirit on Pentecost, who set out to preach the Good News to all the world. As Moreau sent French men and women religious to America, so too do Holy Cross colleges and universities today emulate that spirit by instilling within students a passion for service, whether through volunteering at a local Catholic Worker house or through spending a summer teaching in a Ugandan grade school.

While Holy Cross was young, still fledgling and uncertain of its future in France, Moreau began sending, generously and some might say recklessly, some of his most promising religious out to distant lands. The community's first venture outside France was to Algeria in 1840, only three years after the Congregation was founded. That mission failed after a brief time; however, the first group sent to the United States arrived in 1841, established itself a year later in northern Indiana, and founded the University of Notre Dame, from which many schools, parishes, and other works would eventually be founded. The same fruitfulness took hold in Canada just a few years later: once Holy Cross religious reached Montreal, the community began to grow quickly and spread widely throughout the country. The first missionaries to East Bengal (now Bangladesh) in the following decade struggled mightily, suffering numerous deaths, but persevered. Today, of nine Bangladeshi bishops, five are Holy Cross religious, and the Congregation is proceeding with plans to establish a new college in the Diocese of Mymensingh.

By the mid-1850s, Moreau was receiving more invitations than he could possibly accept to send religious near and far. Invitations came from Martinique, Haiti, Greece, India, Scotland, Argentina, and Poland (where Moreau did send personnel, though the mission foundered), in addition to numerous other French dioceses. No longer was Holy Cross such a shaky proposition. In 1857, the Congregation received its official approbation as a religious institute from Rome, and by then Moreau had clarified its threefold purpose: (1) the perfection of its members through the practice of the evangelical counsels (the vows of chastity, poverty, and obedience); (2) the sanctification of others through preaching, particularly in rural areas and foreign missions; and (3) the Christian instruction and education of youth in schools and orphanages.

Ironically, Moreau, who had sacrificed his earlier dream of becoming a missionary and gave almost half his life to expanding Holy Cross, visited the foundations he supported in Canada and the United States only once, in the same year the community received Pope Pius IX's approval. The young seminarian who burned with passion for reestablishing the Catholic faith in the parishes of western France had grasped Holy Cross's potential as an international apostolic community and seized upon multiple opportunities to increase its reach. That spirit embedded itself within the fabric of the Congregation and led it in the twentieth century, long after Moreau's death, to send religious to Haiti, Central and South America, India, and Africa to found schools and parishes. Holy Cross religious of this era would readily grant the tension that the founder faced and that exists to this day as a result of the missionary impulse to expand and embrace new missions even when the human and financial resources to sustain them are lacking. As dedicated as the Congregation is to education as a primary means of exercising its ministry, it was the call to evangelize in the name of Christ that motivated Moreau and continues to fuel the community's sense of mission.

Moreau was also faulted later, with some justification, for sending community members out into teaching assignments and parishes without adequate religious formation or supervision. He repeatedly stretched the community to the limit of its capacities because he could not bear to know that there were people uneducated and unformed in the faith. The *Constitutions* state that the "mission sends us across borders of every sort,"[13] national, cultural, and linguistic, and the Congregation invites students, parents, parishioners, and coworkers to join in its apostolic work. Whatever the flaws in Moreau's approach, Holy Cross began as a missionary community that also engaged others who were not vowed religious to share in its purposes, and it has continued to serve the Church as such.

Fr. Edward Sorin, C.S.C., the founder of Notre Dame, captured that spirit quite well in a letter he wrote to Moreau less than two weeks after he and seven brothers first arrived in the winter of 1842 at the property located adjacent to

South Bend, Indiana. Sorin and his small band had stepped ashore in New York barely a year earlier, possessing little money or knowledge of the English language. Nevertheless, he boldly predicted, "Before long [Notre Dame] will develop on a large scale. . . . It will be one of the most powerful means for good in this country."[14]

Throughout his life Moreau continued to come up with new ideas and ways to spread the Gospel, and he did not hesitate to send out others to carry out that mission. Some of those efforts failed while others have endured and prospered far beyond any reasonable expectations. At Sainte-Croix his pupils used atlases to track the religious men and women who crossed the Atlantic, and they devoured the letters and tales they sent back. Today air travel allows students to fly across oceans and continents within a day to serve in other countries. Moreau's zeal set an immediate example for Sorin and other missionaries, but the students currently being educated at Holy Cross institutions constitute the founder's greatest legacy. They are the living testimonies to the endurance of his charism—to fuel young people with the passion for venturing out into the world to make God known, loved, and served.

FAMILY

༄

Let us, then, stand in closely united
ranks and, far from separating and
scattering, let us live in such a manner that, as it sees the members of our
family, the world may say of us as the
Gentiles said of the first Christians:
"See how they love one another!"
—*Circular Letters of the Very Reverend
Basil Antony Mary Moreau*, 170

Zeal is the hoped-for product of Christian education in
the two most influential environments of a young person's life: home and school. These places are where they
spend most of their formative years, learning, not just from
parents and mentors but also from siblings, other relatives,
and peers, about what to think and how to act. Moreau
realized that he would never have become a priest but for
the influence of his family, along with his pastor, who first
recognized the stirrings of a vocation and arranged for his
education.

His approach to moral training, like that of his parents, contrasted dramatically with that of the typical nine-
teenth-century school, which was characterized by iron
discipline, including corporal punishment and little toler-
ance for even minor acts of misbehavior. If people associated

with Holy Cross today speak frequently about the "family-like" atmosphere they encounter in our parishes and educational institutions, that is directly traceable to the combination of Moreau's teaching philosophy and ideals for community life. Modeling each group within the Congregation—priests, brothers, and sisters—upon the image of the Holy Family, he also applied those expectations to interactions with students and laity. Moreau cultivated an environment at Sainte-Croix in which both religious and lay faculty were called to be "spiritual parents," and in an unusual step for the time, he formed both a parent advisory committee and an early form of alumni association for graduates, who not surprisingly were known for their devotion to Moreau and Sainte-Croix. In short, he wanted the atmosphere of his school to imitate the good Christian home in which he had been raised. In 1858, a former student who had graduated ten years earlier saw Moreau coming out of the school chapel. He wrote:

> My heart was all a-flutter, like one who sees his aged father once more after a long absence, and I ran toward him. . . . I let myself be caught up in his arms. . . . For me Father Moreau was not an officer of the university who had been in command of the little regiment to which I had belonged, but he was a father who had admitted me within the inner circles of his beloved family and who loved me as a child over a long period of years. . . . For them [priests and brothers], it is not enough simply to throw out a few lessons

in literature or science like so much fodder, but
they see in young men hearts to form and souls
to save.[15]

Most constituents today typically identify that familial
atmosphere as the distinguishing and most appealing fea-
ture of a Holy Cross apostolate. It is, however, an ephemeral
quality, felt more easily by people who have experienced
it than it is readily describable, even for those who have
enjoyed a long association with the Congregation. Any
attempt to articulate the spirit of Holy Cross to someone
who has not been educated in one of its institutions is like
trying to explain the interior dynamics of one's own home
to an acquaintance.

While the concept of family was central to Moreau's
vision, relatively few people appreciate that the personal
attention to students and close collaboration with the laity
characteristic of the community's ministries today, whatever
their own particular qualities, is directly traceable to his
pastoral genius. Moreau referred constantly to the "family"
of Sainte-Croix in his addresses and correspondence and
used the same term in reference to the community at Notre
Dame long before he ever laid eyes upon it. Fr. Sorin, whom
Moreau correctly identified as having the best potential for
leadership among his first group of young priests, imitated
the founder's example and heeded his counsel that priests
and brothers not only teach students but live among them
in dormitories. Not accidentally, the most notable characteristic of "the Notre Dame family" for those who have actually attended the University (and not merely experienced it

vicariously through its athletic program) is the community
spirit and faith life that thrive within its residence halls.

In 1844, Moreau wrote in a short guide for teachers,
"Our students are destined to live in the business and problems of the world. So they should not be made to live a
type of life that they would have to abandon when they
leave our institution. They should be trained in such a way
that they may be everywhere what they were in school."[16]
Though Moreau has never received the credit he deserves
for inspiring it, his vision of forming an enduring sense of
Christian family would come to be the primary takeaway
for students at Sainte-Croix and generations of students in
Holy Cross educational institutions since—the feeling that
alumni of Holy Cross educational institutions instinctively
pick up on and value when they return as graduates, even
after absences of many years.

However, despite his fondness for and ease at relating
to students even as he grew older, Moreau did not encourage
excessive familiarity in his teachers. Neither did he underes-
timate the difficulties of dealing with young people; rather
he urged instructors to be patient with them. It is startling,
given the standard practices of the day, to read the following words in *Christian Education*: "Teachers must keep their
vigilance within reasonable limits and not imitate those who
are always in a state of great alarm, often over some childish
prank which they are unable to evaluate correctly. Those
who are too vigilant are unaware that a great talent of good
teachers is often to pretend not to notice what he or she does
not want to be obliged to punish. An indulgence prudently

managed is worth much more than outbursts and the punishments that follow them. Always avoid this embarrassing vigilance."[17]

Loving the child and sparing the rod while resisting the temptation to act like a buddy would be good ABCs for any teacher's manual or simply good advice for parents today. The language may be slightly archaic, but the general principles are translatable to primary schools and college classrooms and dormitories. Moreau recognized the need to maintain a deliberate balance between firmness and leniency in dealing with students. He intuitively understood the difference between a teacher-mentor and a hovering ninny. Good teachers avoid fighting small battles and liberate their students to soar rather than quashing their spirits. He relished being around young people and, unlike some teachers, chose to be amused rather than irritated by their smaller follies.

Moreau took the principles of religious formation that he refined over the course of years spent as a seminary professor and mentor and combined those with a thoroughly enlightened, modern, pragmatic approach to education. But he was also naturally warm-hearted and indelibly influenced by parents who built their household upon the twin pillars of love and faith. In some sense, he sought to replicate that environment in both the structure of his religious community and the type of education he provided to students in and outside the classroom. His generosity and kindness infused Sainte-Croix with a familial spirit that made it, unusually for its era, both a school and a home. He loved students; they knew it; and it changed how they lived once they left the school walls behind.

HOPE

❦

Human life is only a long way of the cross. It is not necessary to enter the chapel or the church to run over the various stations. The way of the cross is everywhere, and we walk along it every day in spite of ourselves and often unknown to us.

—1857 *Conference to Sisters*

Next to the Chapel of Christ the Teacher at the University of Portland stands a bell tower erected in 2009. The Congregational motto, *Ave Crux Spes Unica* (Hail the Cross, Our Only Hope), is carved across the entrance at its base. Atop its peak stands a cross with a small glass globe in the middle that causes it to cast both light and shadow simultaneously. This cross captures the central paradox that catapults Christians into another reality—the conviction that the Son of God died willingly, even for the sake of those who persecuted and abandoned him, in order to bring us through darkness to glory.

When Moreau wrote in 1849 that "Jesus Christ should be our model, since our likeness to this divine master is the foundation of our predestination to eternal glory,"[18] he expressed simply the heart of the Christian's call. Striving for completeness means spending one's life as a citizen of this world in imitating the person of Christ as the gateway to citizenship in heaven. On this bedrock principle, all faith and thus all human hope rests. A Christian is compelled then to be zealous for union with God and to direct his or her thoughts and actions accordingly. While it is possible for a person to navigate his own path without formal or substantial instruction in the faith, as was true of Moreau's parents, some leaders—lay, religious, and clergy—must be capable of articulating and teaching the message of the Gospel. Consequently, the work of education is essential to the life of the Church and its mission of going out to all the nations proclaiming the Gospel, as Jesus instructed his disciples to do in his final commission.

Eighteen hundred years later, Moreau looked upon the spiritual wreckage of his native France and felt called to become an educator in the faith. As his vision and heart expanded, he followed the apostolic example of sending out missionaries to give their lives over to the founding of parishes and schools. He expected instructors, whether religious or lay, to cultivate excellence in the classroom, be models of zealous virtue, and fashion a second home for their charges. As would any Catholic educator, he wanted those young people to carry their formation with them and be battle-ready for the challenges to their faith that they would inevitably face in the wider world.

Still, the first four principles of mind, heart, zeal, and family, important though they are, would have little distinctive Christian purpose apart from hope in the Cross of Christ. They constitute the foundation of an education in the faith, but a person's capacity for lifelong discipleship is hard to predict from exam results or résumés no matter how well formed he or she may be. Moreau prayed that students would remember what they were at Sainte-Croix—and other Holy Cross schools—and live the same everywhere, but ultimately he could only hope that they would persevere in faith once they graduated and entered upon their long journeys back to the Father.

One does not have to be a Christian to believe that adversity does, or at least can, make people stronger and prepare them for harder challenges in the future, but no education in the faith is complete without an understanding of how the Cross is much more than a burden once carried by Jesus. It was for Moreau "a treasure more valuable than gold and precious stones."[19] In both light and shadow, the Cross is Christ's gift to us, our only hope. Moreau's trust in the Cross is the essential component of his legacy, and its influence can be found in the final section of the Congregation's *Constitutions*, written more than a century after his death: "We must be men with hope to bring. There is no failure the Lord's love cannot reverse, no humiliation he cannot exchange for blessing, no anger he cannot dissolve, no routine he cannot transfigure. All is swallowed up in victory. He has nothing but gifts to offer. It remains only for us to find how even the cross can be borne as a gift."[20]

From its foundation in 1837, the Congregation has faced a litany of crosses—financial crises; political unrest; religious persecution; deaths of religious from disease, natural disasters, and violence; and the waywardness of others.

As the father of Holy Cross, Moreau experienced many of these trials personally, but through them all, both congregational and personal, he always encouraged the community to see the hand of Divine Providence. He firmly believed that the Lord's choicest blessings come through the crosses we bear out of love for him and love for others. The paradox of the Cross is a hard truth to accept but one that is therefore even more necessary to model and teach.

Yet none of us does that alone, including those whose mission lies in Christian education. A line in the *Constitutions* reads, "And, as in every work of our mission, we find that we ourselves stand to learn much from those whom we are called to teach."[21] Christians spread hope, and religious, like those in Holy Cross, have a special obligation to embolden others to pick up their crosses. Yet we too draw strength from the family spirit in our institutions and are better disciples when humble enough to admit that we have a lot to learn from students and coworkers of all ages. For all our learning, we seek a deeper wisdom. We yearn to look out upon the world like the awestruck shepherds who gazed in wonder at Mary's newborn son and, during more difficult times, to emulate the friends who stood by her decades later as she stared up at his Cross, willing herself to trust in God's promise.

The educational process itself requires a particular type of dying to self. Whenever we have to shed old ways of thinking, viewing, or perceiving the world around us and ourselves, a conversion of both heart and mind must take place. The contemplation of new ideas and needs beyond our comfort zones requires a sacrificial willingness to put at risk everything that we think we already know. We need to have hope in that process in order to stick with it, to trust the natural impulses of our hearts and believe that what is born of questioning beliefs previously taken for granted will lead us to a new and better understanding of our vocation as citizens in this world and the next.

The charism of education in the faith that the Holy Spirit entrusted to the Congregation of Holy Cross through Blessed Basil Moreau combines a form of pedagogy that mirrors a person's natural human development and moral formation with the call to Christian discipleship. It encourages believers to embrace the Cross of Jesus while progressing through this world toward the light of God's kingdom. Whether through the recognition that time is always shorter than we think or the lasting effects of Moreau's own missionary impulses, Holy Cross religious today are still formed with the sense of urgency found in the conclusion of *Christian Education*: "Make haste, therefore; take up this work of the resurrection, never forgetting that the particular goal of your institute is, above all, to sanctify youth. By this, you will contribute to preparing the world for better times than our own, for these children who today attend your school are the parents of the future and the parents of future generations."[22]

Mind. Heart. Zeal. Family. Hope.
Ave Crux Spes Unica!

Appendix I: Holy Cross Chronology

∽

1799 Basil Moreau born as French Revolution ends.

1814 Moreau enters minor seminary in Le Mans, France.

1820 Fr. Jacques Dujarié founds Brothers of St. Joseph.

1821 Moreau ordained a priest.

1825 Moreau begins eleven-year appointment as theology professor at St. Vincent Seminary.

1835 Moreau takes over responsibility for Brothers, assembles small group of auxiliary priests.

1836 Moreau opens primary boarding school at Sainte-Croix.

1837 Fifty-four brothers and seven auxiliary priests sign a "Fundamental Act of Union," marking the founding of Holy Cross as a religious community.

1840 First overseas mission founded in Algeria.

1841 Moreau founds Marianites (sisters) of Holy Cross.

1842 Indiana mission founds University of Notre Dame.

1847 Holy Cross establishes Canadian mission in Montreal.

1852 Mission to East Bengal (Bangladesh) accepted.

1856 Moreau writes *Christian Education*.

1857 Congregation of Holy Cross formally approved by Rome. Moreau makes only visit to North America.

1866 Moreau resigns as Superior General.

1871 Moreau celebrates fiftieth anniversary of ordination.

1873 Moreau dies.

1878 St. Edward's University in Austin, Texas, founded.

1902 Holy Cross accepts responsibility for the University of Portland.

1943 Holy Cross founds first missions to South America in Chile and Brazil.

1944 Holy Cross arrives in Haiti.

1946 King's College in Wilkes-Barre, Pennsylvania, founded.

1948 Stonehill College in Easton, Massachusetts, founded.

1958 Holy Cross arrives in Ghana and Uganda.

1959 Missionaries from Canada arrive in South India.

1978 Holy Cross enters Kenya.

1987 First parish established in Monterrey, Mexico.

2000 First parish established in Tanzania.

2007 Blessed Basil Moreau beatified by Pope Benedict XVI.

2008 Religious from India open house in Philippines.

Appendix II: Anthology of Quotations on Christian Education

∽

The publication of *Basil Moreau: Essential Writings* in 2014 has helped immeasurably in compiling many of his most well-known and important works into a single volume. A great deal of Moreau's work has also been made available through the efforts of The Holy Cross Institute at St. Edward's University in Austin, Texas (http://www.holycrossinstitute. org/resources/writings). Both of these are listed under the "Further Reading" section that follows. The quotes that follow rely mainly upon those two sources.

However, many of Moreau's writings have yet to be translated from their original French. Others exist merely as fragments or can be found only by scouring through secondary literature. In some cases, references are actually confusing. For example, he wrote a number of "meditations," but also used the word as a title (e.g., "Meditations" or "Christian Meditations"). Even his main work, *Christian Education*, is referred to as *Christian Pedagogy* by some, though the former has recently gained more general acceptance, at least in the United States. And because there is no authorized corpus of Moreau's works, different translations of the same writings are in circulation.

Despite these obstacles, the more one reads of Moreau, the clearer it becomes that he was a gifted scholar with a deep understanding of scripture and an ability to articulate his interpretations cogently. There are gems in his writings that reveal a timeless understanding of human nature. His reputation as an educator has certainly grown over the last several decades, but *The Theology of Basil Moreau* is a book that still needs to be written. Like this selection of quotes, it may be hard to gather together, but the founder of Holy Cross had a unified theological framework that well merits deeper study. I hope that the material in this booklet will encourage even more research into him as both an educator and a theologian.

From Moreau's *Christian Education*

Education is the art of helping young people to completeness.

୨

I have always been convinced that the first duty of any teacher is to produce Christians; society has a greater need for people of values than it has for scholars.

୨

In order to succeed in acquiring a superior degree of knowledge, teachers must have a constant desire for self-improvement and lose no opportunity to satisfy this ambition when it is not detrimental to their other duties.

୨

Zeal is the great desire to make God known, loved, and served, and thus to bring knowledge of salvation to others.

୨

If at times you show preference to any young person, it should be the poor, those who have no one else to show them preference, those who have the least knowledge, those who lack skills and talent, and those who are not Catholic or Christian. If you show them greater care and concern, it must be because their needs are greater and because it is only just to give more to those who have received less.

☉

Teachers must keep their vigilance within reasonable limits and not imitate those who are always in a state of great alarm, often over some childish prank that they are unable to evaluate correctly. Those who are too vigilant are unaware that a great talent of good teachers is often to pretend not to notice what he or she does not want to be obliged to punish. An indulgence prudently managed is worth much more than outbursts and the punishments that follow them.

☉

Anyone who knows young people easily recognizes the necessity of patience, which is the only thing that permits a teacher to rise above the difficulties inherent in educating youth.

☉

Never forget that all teaching lies in the best approach to an individual student, that all successes you find will be in direct proportion to the efforts you have made in this area.

☉

Make haste, therefore; take up this work of the resurrection, never forgetting that the particular goal of your institution is, above all, to sanctify youth. By this, you will contribute to preparing the world for better times than our own, for these children who today attend your school are the parents of the future and the parents of future generations.

Other Quotes on Education

An education that is complete is one in which the hands and heart are engaged as much as the mind. We want to let our students try their learning in the world and so make prayers of their educations.

☙

Our students are destined to live in the business and problems of the world. So they should not be made to live a type of life that they would have to abandon when they leave our institution. They should be trained in such a way that they may be everywhere what they were in school.

☙

Great teachers are courageous and unshakable and tender and compassionate, like Jesus Christ, the model of all teachers, who loved to be bothered by young people. Without this zeal among teachers, everything falls apart.

From Moreau's *Circular Letters*

If education was ever a difficult work from the Christian viewpoint, it is assuredly so today, when parents almost seem leagued together to ruin our young people by raising them in the school of a world wrapped up in materialism.

☙

Even though we base our philosophy course on the data of faith, no one need fear that we shall confine our teaching within narrow and unscientific boundaries. No, we wish to accept science without prejudice and in a manner adapted to the needs of our times. We do not want our students to be ignorant of anything they should know. To this end, we shall shrink from no sacrifice. But we shall never forget that virtue, as Bacon, puts it, is the spice which preserves science. We shall always place education side by side with instruction; the mind will not be cultivated at the expense of the heart. While we prepare useful citizens for society, we shall likewise do our utmost to prepare citizens for heaven.

☙

To succeed in the important undertaking entrusted to us, we must be, first of all, so closely united in charity as to form but one mind and one soul.

☙

What is true of a palace whose foundations have been laid and which is rising gradually until completion is verified, likewise, in a great work of charity. It is not one alone who builds; nor is it one stone, or one single beam of wood, that forms it. Each worker contributes something from his own trade; each stone is cut to fit into its one appointed place; and each piece of wood is arranged and placed so as to enhance the general effect of the entire building. Union, then, is a powerful lever with which we could move, direct, and sanctify the whole world, if the spirit of evil, who has been allowed to exercise his power over this earth, does not set himself up against the wondrous effects of this moral force.

For those who live by faith, the cross is a treasure more valuable than gold and precious stones.

We are in greater need than ever before of renewing ourselves in the spirit of our vocation. Let us not forget that the development of the work entrusted to us depends upon our acceptance of the inspirations of grace and our fidelity in seconding the designs of Divine Providence. For the future, then, far from dwelling with vain complacency on any success achieved thus far, let us humble ourselves for the hindrances which we may have placed, even inadvertently, in the way of still greater success, and let us strive with complete self-distrust to consolidate and perfect what has been begun.

In fact, it is in meditation on the great truths of our faith that we learn to detach ourselves from the swiftly passing shadow of the world, which like a rushing torrent, carries off in its waves both people and goods. It is in such meditation that we train ourselves to see the hand of God in all the events of life.

If I could have foreseen the development of the Congregation of Holy Cross from the outset, I could then have regulated and coordinated everything in advance. If such were the case, however, the Congregation would have been a merely human combination and not the work of Divine Providence.

The fact of the matter is that it began and developed in a manner so mysterious, that I can claim for myself neither credit for its foundation nor merit for its progress. Therein lies the indubitable proof that God alone is the Founder of this Congregation, since, according to St. Augustine, when we cannot find the cause of a good work, we must recognize that the Lord is its beginning and author.

From Moreau's Sermons, Spiritual Exercises, and Other Writings

We become what we think upon, and so it is particularly necessary that we learn how to meditate well.

What must we do to become perfect? Follow Jesus Christ, that is to say, imitate him; that is the commitment we made in baptism. . . . Following Jesus is the consequence of this sacrament of faith; it is the holy and irrevocable law of our vocation to Christianity, and we renew it by our religious promises. In what does this imitation of Jesus Christ consist? He himself told us that it is reduced to three things: renouncing ourselves, taking up our cross, and walking in his footsteps.

If faith is not found in the ministers of the gospel, where on earth will we ever find it?

Pride is not only the greatest enemy to true union with God; it is also the greatest enemy to the true community spirit.

Of all the passions that tyrannize over us, the passion for esteem is the most common because it constantly pursues every one of us. . . . It waits forever at the door of the heart, watching its chance for entrance.

Where all the members of a house are humble, there can be but few sins against charity.

Your whole life should have as its aim to so well assimilate the thoughts, judgments, desires, words, and actions of Jesus Christ that you can say with the great Apostle: "I no longer live, it is Christ who lives in me."

The sacraments are the most tangible proof of the love of Jesus Christ for us.

To go to confession means to let a conscience speak.

If we consider the Sacred Heart relative to ourselves, we see it as the heart of our friend, our brother, our father, and our Savior.

Unless you imitate Jesus Christ, you cannot truly be a Christian.

Love then Jesus Christ and before long his thoughts, conduct, actions, and affections will be yours.

_☉_

Is it an exaggeration to say with the saints that the heart of our God on the altar is a blazing furnace? That it is a burning hearth from which there continually comes forth a sacred fire to set our souls on fire?

_☉_

The wine of [Jesus'] love inebriates my heart, and the bread of your charity strengthens it.

_☉_

We are committed by our vocation to extend the reign of Jesus Christ in the hearts of all people.

_☉_

If the struggle is rough and difficult, the victory will be sweet, and the peace eternal.

_☉_

The Eucharist is the heart of Christian charity, absolute and universal. . . . The charity of Jesus in the Church knows no limitation.

_☉_

The priest is bound to become learned, not merely for his own sake but that of others also. . . . Nothing is sadder than a mediocre priest.

_☉_

Do not forget that Christianity is above all a practical religion. Admire its poetry, for it is sublime; but study its Ten Commandments, for they lead to heaven.

ᘓ

Human life is like a great way of the cross. We do not have to go to the chapel or church to go through the different stations. This way of the cross is everywhere and we travel it every day, even in spite of ourselves and without being aware of it.

ᘓ

Prayer is like a health zone which we must set up around our homes and schools. Moreover, it alone can heal souls, and it is in souls, much more than in the organs of the body or the elements of nature, that we find the causes of the physical and moral evils which are today playing havoc with society.

ᘓ

If you consider your own vocation, whether it be that of priest, or parent of a family, is there one that by its nature demands more work? Don't you all have to work ceaselessly to care for the flock entrusted to you, giving it all your attention, your concern, sacrificing your time, your rest, your health and finally your whole life?

From the *Constitutions of the Congregation of Holy Cross*

8. We wished to abandon all to follow Christ. We learned in time that we still had it within ourselves to hold back. We wish to be wholehearted yet we are hesitant. Still, like

the first disciples we know that He will draw us along and reinforce our loyalties if we yield to Him.

☙

14. For the kingdom to come in this world, disciples must have the competence to see and the courage to act.

☙

16. For many of us in Holy Cross, mission expresses itself in the education of youth in schools, colleges, and universities. For others, our mission as educators takes place in parishes and other ministries. Wherever we work we assist others not only to recognize and develop their own gifts but also to discover the deepest longing in their lives. And, as in every work of our mission, we find that we ourselves stand to learn much from those whom we are called to teach.

☙

17. Our mission sends us across borders of every sort. Often we must make ourselves at home among more than one people or culture, reminding us again that the farther we go in giving the more we stand to receive. Our broader experience allows both the appreciation and the critique of every culture and the disclosure that no culture of this world can be our abiding home.

☙

34. We grow close to one another as brothers by living together in community. If we do not love the brothers whom we see, then we cannot love the God whom we have not seen.

☙

42. It is essential to our mission that we strive to abide so attentively together that people will observe: "See how they love one another." We will then be a sign in an alienated world: men who have, for love of their Lord, become closest neighbors, trustworthy friends, brothers.

☉

118. We must be men with hope to bring. There is no failure the Lord's love cannot reverse, no humiliation he cannot exchange for blessing, no anger he cannot dissolve, no routine he cannot transfigure. All is swallowed up in victory. He has nothing but gifts to offer. It remains only for us to find how even the cross can be borne as a gift.

☉

122. The footsteps of those men who called us to walk in their company left deep prints, as of men carrying heavy burdens. But they did not trudge; they strode. For they had the hope.

Appendix III: Prayers

∾

Prayer for the Family of Holy Cross (I)

Almighty God,
source of light and glory,
through the gospel of Jesus Christ and the Family of Holy
    Cross
you have called us to make your truth and justice known.

Like the stars in the heavens,
may we extend your light throughout the world,
a world enslaved by injustice and war,
hatred, mistrust, and division.

May our example and teaching
be a means to transform minds and hearts,
to prepare the world for better times,
for the coming of your reign.

Empower us with hope in your glory,
so we can remain faithful
and complete the work you have entrusted to us.
We ask this through Christ Jesus, our Lord.
Amen.

Prayer for the Family of Holy Cross (II)

Provident God,
you inspired Basil Moreau

to form a family of three societies,
men and women, lay and ordained,
to be a sign of love and unity in a world of division.
May we, as brothers, sisters, and priests in Holy Cross,
be more closely joined in our bond of mutual charity
and in fidelity to our vows,
for in unity is our strength.

We pray that our witness of mutual respect and shared
    undertaking
will be a hopeful sign of the kingdom,
where others can behold how we love one another.

Bless and strengthen our collaborative efforts, our shared
    mission,
and our communion of vocation,
that like a mighty tree,
Holy Cross will grow and spring forth
new limbs and branches around the world,
bringing hope, justice, and love to those in need.
We pray this through Jesus Christ, our Lord and brother.
Amen.

Prayer for the Family of Holy Cross (III)

Lord God,
you inspired our founder, Basil Moreau,
to establish the religious Family of Holy Cross
and to call us to live and work together
as "a visible imitation of the Holy Family."
The common life and work of Holy Cross

was to be "a powerful lever with which to move,
direct, and sanctify the world."
Enable in your Family of Holy Cross
a deeper fidelity to the founding vision of Basil Moreau
so we might be a sign of God's love
and tender mercy to people everywhere.
We ask this through Christ, our Lord.
Amen.

Prayer for the Intercession of Blessed Moreau

Lord Jesus,
source of all that is good,
you inspired Basil Moreau
to found the religious Family of Holy Cross
to continue your mission among the People of God.
May he be for us a model of apostolic life,
an example of fidelity,
and an inspiration as we strive to follow you.
Lord Jesus,
you said, "Ask and you shall receive."
We come to ask you that you hear our prayer.
It is through the intercession of Basil Moreau that we ask . . .
(state your intention)
May we learn to imitate his holiness and service
and look to him confidently in times of need.
Amen.

NOTES

1. Etienne Catta and Tony Catta, *Basil Anthony Mary Moreau*, trans. by Edward L. Heston, 2 vols. (Milwaukee: Bruce, 1955), 1:142.

2. Basil Moreau, *Basil Moreau: Essential Writings*, eds. Kevin Grove, C.S.C., and Andrew Gawrych, C.S.C. (Notre Dame, IN: Ave Maria Press, 2014), 333.

3. John Henry Newman, *The Idea of a University* (Washington, DC: Regnery Press, 1999), 165.

4. Basil Moreau, *Circular Letters of the Very Reverend Basil Antony Mary Moreau: Founder of the Religious of Holy Cross*, ed. Joel Giallanza, C.S.C., and Jacques Grisé, C.S.C. (Rome: Congregazione di Santa Croce, 1998), xx.

5. Congregation of Holy Cross, *Constitutions of the Congregation of Holy Cross* (Rome: Congregation of Holy Cross, 1988), 2.15.

6. Quoted in Catta and Catta, *Basil Anthony Mary Moreau*, 1:53.

7. Basil Moreau, "*Sermons*, 'The Rule,' 1833," in "From the Writings of Father Basil Anthony Moreau, Founder of the Congregation of Holy Cross," http://www.holycrossinstitute.org/resources/writings.

8. From the King's College vision statement, http://www.kings.edu/aboutkings/traditions_and_mission/mission_statement.

9. John Paul II, *Ex Corde Ecclesiae* (Vatican City: Libreria Editrice Vaticana, 1990), 23.

10, Moreau, *Essential Writings*, 338.

11. Ibid., 337.

12. Basil Moreau, "1855 Exercises, 'Meditation for the Feast of the Patronage of St. Joseph,'" in "From the Writings of Father Basil Anthony Moreau, Founder of the Congregation of Holy Cross," http://www.holycrossinstitute.org/resources/writings.

13. Congregation of Holy Cross, *Constitutions*, 2.17.

14. Edward Sorin, C.S.C., quoted on the University of Notre Dame website (http://www.nd.edu/about/).

15. Quoted in Catta and Catta, *Basil Anthony Mary Moreau*, 1:641–2.

16. Quoted on the St. Edward's University website http://www.stedwards.edu/holycrosslegacy.

17. Moreau, *Essential Writings*, 340.

18. Ibid., 418.

19. Ibid., 413.

20. Congregation of Holy Cross, *Constitutions*, 8:118.

21. Ibid., 2.16.

22. Moreau, *Essential Writings*, 376.

FURTHER READING

Barrosse, Thomas. *Moreau, Portrait of a Founder*. Notre Dame, IN: Fides Publishers, 1969.

Catta, Etienne, and Tony Catta. *Basil Anthony Mary Moreau*. Translated by Edward L. Heston. 2 vols. Milwaukee: Bruce, 1955.

Congregation of Holy Cross. *Constitutions of the Congregation of Holy Cross*. Rome: Congregation of Holy Cross, 1988.

———. *Directory of Devotional Prayer*. Notre Dame, IN: Ave Maria Press, 2012.

Gawrych, Andrew, C.S.C., and Kevin Grove, C.S.C., eds. *The Cross, Our Only Hope: Daily Reflections in the Holy Cross Tradition*. Notre Dame, IN: Ave Maria Press, 2008.

Giallanza, Joel, C.S.C. *Praying from the Heart of Holy Cross Spirituality: A 30-Day Retreat with Basil Moreau*. Notre Dame, IN: Ave Maria Press, 2010.

Holy Cross Institute at St. Edwards University. *Resource Center: Writings and Reflections*. http://www.holycrossinstitute.org/resources/writings.

John Paul II. "Apostolic Constitution *Ex Corde Ecclesiae*." Vatican City: Libreria Editrice Vaticana, 1990. http://w2.vatican.va/content/john-paul-ii/en/apost_constitutions/documents/hf_jp-ii_apc_15081990_ex-corde-ecclesiae.html.

MacEoin, Gary. *Father Moreau: Founder of Holy Cross*. Milwaukee: Bruce, 1962. Republished as *Basil Moreau: Founder of Holy Cross*. Notre Dame, IN: Ave Maria Press, 2007.

Moreau, Basil. *Basil Moreau: Essential Writings*. Edited by Kevin Grove, C.S.C., and Andrew Gawrych, C.S.C. Notre Dame, IN: Ave Maria Press, 2014.

————. *Christian Education*. Austin, TX: Holy Cross Institute at St. Edward's University, 2006.

————. *Circular Letters of the Very Reverend Basil Antony Mary Moreau: Founder of the Religious of Holy Cross*. Edited by Joel Giallanza, C.S.C., and Jacques Grisé, C.S.C. Rome: Congregazione di Santa Croce, 1998.

Newman, John Henry. *The Idea of a University*. Washington, DC: Regnery Press, 1999.

IN THE HOLY CROSS TRADITION

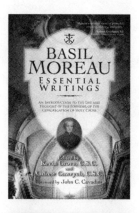

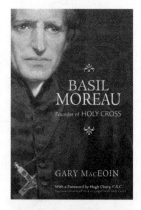

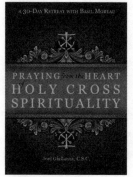

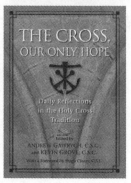